Original title:
The Meaning of Life, One Joke at a Time

Author: Helena Marchant
ISBN HARDBACK: 978-1-80566-184-9
ISBN PAPERBACK: 978-1-80566-479-6

Riddles of the Infinite

Why did the chicken flee the street?
A riddle's joy is quite the treat!
For every puzzle that we face,
A giggle hides in every place.

What's the secret of the sun?
A ray of fun, it's just begun!
With every laugh, we break the mold,
Eternal jests, like tales of old.

A Jest for Every Journey

Pack your bags with puns and cheer,
Each step along, let laughter steer.
A joyful heart makes little fuss,
Each joke a compass, guiding us.

In every corner, find the quirk,
A stumble turns to playful perk.
With every mile, let humor bloom,
A jestous path, dispelling gloom.

Smirk at the Stars

Look up high, what do you see?
Twinkling lights, and giggles free!
Each star a wink, a wink so bright,
A cosmic joke that lights the night.

They say the moon's a big old pie,
A slice of joy that floats on high.
So whisper dreams up to the sky,
And let your laughter dance and fly.

Whimsy and Wisdom Intertwined

In the garden of quirky thoughts,
Wisdom blooms with funny knots.
A chuckle here, a snicker there,
Expressions of joy, floating in air.

With every moment, life can tease,
So take a breath and laugh with ease.
In whimsy found, we play the muse,
A guiding light that we all choose.

Smirks and Epiphanies

In a world of mundane grind,
A chuckle's all we need to find.
With every twist of fate we see,
Laughter's key to set us free.

Why take life so very serious?
Jokes are wondrous, quite mysterious.
Every giggle holds a clue,
To happiness, just me and you.

When trouble knocks upon our door,
Just tickle it, then laugh some more.
For wisdom hides in silly puns,
And joy is found in playful runs.

So dance with glee through ups and downs,
Wear laughter bright, erase those frowns.
For life's a jest, delightful, bold,
In every laugh, our hearts unfold.

Life's Whimsical Tapestry

Threads of joy, a funny weave,
Each snicker hides a little reprieve.
A tapestry of gags and quips,
That makes us smile, as laughter grips.

Frogs in suits and cats with hats,
Conversations with playful spats.
Every silly tale does show,
Life's vibrant dance, a grandioso.

Through tickles and delightful sighs,
The world unfolds in playful highs.
Wander through this merry land,
With jokes to guide us, hand in hand.

So let's paint life with shades of cheer,
Where laughter's echoes are always near.
In every stitch, a tale we find,
Life's whimsy crafted, sweetly designed.

Reflections of Joy through Jests

In mirrors bright, reflections play,
With jesters dancing in the fray.
A wink, a nod—what do you see?
Just silly smiles, us being free.

Life's puzzle pieces fit just right,
When jokes unlock those beams of light.
A pun is like a gentle hug,
That wraps around, cozy and snug.

So share a laugh, let worries fade,
With humor, happiness is made.
In every chuckle, wisdom lays,
A brightened heart transforms our days.

Each jest a mirror to embrace,
Bringing warmth, familiar grace.
For in this dance of witty wit,
Our joy ignites, and never quits.

The Sassy Essence of Being

In the sass of life, we twirl and sway,
With laughter lighting up the way.
Every quip, a spark divine,
In silly moments, we align.

Why dwell on woes that drag us down?
Let's wear our smiles, discard the frown.
With every pun that breezes through,
Life struts its stuff, a funky view.

Witty banter, snappy lines,
Crafting joy, where laughter shines.
We're the jesters, bold and free,
Embracing life's absurdity.

So raise a glass to all that's funny,
For laughter makes the world less runny.
In sassy tales, we find delight,
Life's essence glows, forever bright.

Joyful Journeys in Jest

With a wink and a grin, we set sail,
Counting giggles, we never fail.
Life's a ride on a twirling cart,
Joy blooms brightly, a playful art.

In the bustling crowd, a clown appears,
Tickling laughter, easing our fears.
Each step we take, a punchline found,
Joyful journeys, where laughs abound.

Silly moments dance in our hearts,
Life's a puzzle with quirky parts.
In every mishap, there's fun to see,
Jests and japes set our spirits free.

So join the parade, let laughter lead,
Sowing the sunshine like a wild seed.
With each chuckle, a bond we share,
Joyful journeys, love everywhere.

The Art of Laughing in Life.

A tickle here, a nudge over there,
Life's little quirks are beyond compare.
Each smirk a brushstroke on the page,
Crafting joy, no matter the stage.

In the canvas of life, humor blends,
Rolling with laughter, making new friends.
With each hearty chuckle, we soar,
Art of laughing opens every door.

Stumbles and trips bring joyous delight,
Shadows become light in the late night.
Every faux pas is just a new chance,
To spin a tale and join the dance.

In every tear, a jest will twirl,
Silly moments unfurl and unfurl.
So grab your smile, let's paint it bright,
The art of laughing makes everything right.

Laughter's Echoes in the Dark

In the quiet night, a giggle breaks,
Echoes of joy in the paths it takes.
Stars winking down, sharing a jest,
In the dark, laughter feels like a quest.

With shadows that dance in silly glee,
We find our joy, just you and me.
Why worry so much? Just let it go,
Laughter's echo is the star of the show.

Tickles and tugs, a fizzy delight,
Belly laughs chasing away the fright.
With every joke, the dark's painted bright,
Silly whispers soft like the moonlight.

So when you feel lost, look for the sound,
Of laughter's echoes that surround.
In the depths of night, we find our spark,
Holding hands tightly, we light the dark.

Whispers of a Cosmic Chuckle

In the vastness, a giggle plays,
The stars chuckle in mysterious ways.
Galaxies spin with a joyful grin,
Cosmic humor bubbles from within.

Comets streak by, grace in each line,
Whispers of laughter, ever divine.
In the dance of the cosmos, we sway,
Finding joy in the grand display.

Planets collide with a playful thud,
Creating a ruckus, a zigzag flood.
In the universe's heart, we find delight,
Cosmic chuckles echo through the night.

So listen closely to the heavens above,
Tune into laughter and twinkle of love.
In this wild expanse, let your spirit soar,
Whispers of joy forever implore.

Laughter in the Shadows

In the dark where chuckles hide,
A banana peel, oh what a ride.
A slip, a trip, we all will see,
Life's little quirks, so wild and free.

Tickles dance behind closed doors,
Muffled giggles, laughter soars.
Each joke a spark, a brilliant light,
In shadows deep, we find delight.

Chuckles of Existence

Why did the chicken cross the street?
To find a nice seat for a fun repeat.
With every step, a giggle emerges,
Life's oddities, how laughter urges.

A jester's cap, a smile so bright,
Every punchline feels just right.
In this play, we act and jest,
Finding joy in every quest.

Jests That Illuminate

Two fish swim, and one starts to joke,
Knocking on wood, just to provoke.
Splashing laughter, bubbles rise,
The simplest things bring sweet surprise.

In the glow of a quirky pun,
We discover how life can be fun.
Each jest a beacon, shining true,
Guiding us, as laughter ensues.

Whispers of Whimsy

A squirrel in a hat, oh what a sight,
Chasing the sun, from morning till night.
With every laugh, a story spins,
In this world, joyful chaos wins.

A jellybean dance, so absurdly sweet,
Life's little moments, a comic feat.
Whispers of whimsy float in the air,
Reminding us all, to simply beware.

Silly Signposts on Life's Journey

A sign that says, 'Turn here for fun,'
But you keep driving, missing the pun.
Life's a park, not just a race,
With squirrels that dance at a frantic pace.

A road marked 'Serious' to avoid a pit,
But you stumble right into a clown's skit.
Each detour filled with giggles and glee,
Navigating life's map is quite the spree.

When you trip on your shoelace and fall with a smack,
Life hands you a mirror; there's laughter to track.
Bumps in the road bear whimsical charms,
Even mishaps can cradle us in warm arms.

So let those signposts point you to cheer,
In a world where jokers always appear.
With each twist and turn, don't forget to smile,
For joy is the journey, and life is worthwhile.

Lively Laughs as Life's Compass

In a compass of chuckles, we dance about,
Sailing through storms with joy, no doubt.
Navigating winters with jokes so bold,
Finding warmth in laughter, more precious than gold.

Each tick of the clock chimes a jest,
Tickle your worries; let laughter be best.
Maps of hilarity drawn in chalk,
Guiding the way, let your spirit talk.

Underneath the stars, a humor parade,
Shadows of seriousness start to fade.
Count your giggles, stack them high,
In this lively journey, let out a sigh.

So grab your compass, let chuckles unfold,
In this funny tale, be vibrant and bold.
With each twist and laugh, you're holding the key,
To navigate through life, wild and free.

The Grin of Gratefulness

A smile's the sun on a cloudy day,
Chasing the gray, sending gloom on its way.
When the world seems heavy, let laughter take flight,
Grateful grins shine even in the night.

Jokes crack like thunder, echoing cheer,
Each punchline a beacon, pulling us near.
The little things matter, like socks on a cat,
Filling us up with joy, just like that.

In the mirror, a joker winks right back,
With silly faces that we never lack.
Life's a dance hall where smiles sway free,
Each chuckle a drop in life's big sea.

To embrace the silly is truly divine,
Gratefulness bubbles in each playful line.
Keep that grin bright, let laughter align,
In a world filled with joy, your heart will shine.

Eclectic Echoes of Amusement

Whispers of joy that tickle the mind,
In quirky echoes, true treasures we find.
Life hums a tune only laughter can sing,
With silly refrains that begin to take wing.

The sound of a giggle, a pop, and a crack,
Each note a reminder, when we lose track.
In laughter's embrace, confusion takes flight,
As jokes sprinkle moments with pure delight.

A carnival song played on a flute,
Turns worries to shadows, a silly pursuit.
Lost in the riddle of laughter's sweet grace,
Discovering joy in a comical space.

So dance in the echoes, be bold and be bright,
In life's eclectic rhythm, find a new light.
With laughter, the journey becomes an art,
A melodious adventure, straight from the heart.

The Punchline of Existence

In a world so full of quirks,
We stumble through our daily works.
Laughter hides in every nook,
Just take a look, just take a look.

A banana peel on the floor,
Leads to giggles, oh, what a score!
Life's a stage with silly roles,
And comedy is what consoles.

With jokes we share, we dance and weave,
Tickling hearts, it's hard to grieve.
The punchline hits, we laugh and cheer,
Together born, we shed a tear.

So grab a friend, let laughter reign,
In every jest, we dodge the pain.
Life's too short to frown or pout,
Let's laugh it up, that's what it's about.

Giggles Beneath the Stars

Beneath the twinkle, a laugh erupts,
As cosmic jest plays, our hearts corrupts.
A shooting star with a wink and a grin,
The universe knows where the fun begins.

Whispers of humor dance in the night,
Turning worries into pure delight.
An owl hoots a wise-crack on cue,
Nature joins in on the giggling too.

A tumble of clouds, a remix of laughs,
Life's a buffet, take a slice of quaffs.
The moon chuckles, the sun gives a nudge,
With each little joke, we plot our grudge.

So let's gather close, beneath the glow,
Share our stories, let the laughter flow.
In giggles wrapped, the cosmos spins,
Finding joy in the silly wins.

Humor in the Shadows of Being

In the shadows, where fears might loom,
A jester's cap, dispelling the gloom.
With a whoopee cushion, we break the ice,
Life's a punchline, oh, isn't that nice?

The riddles of fate play tricks on the wise,
A jest is the path through life's grand disguise.
Look in the mirror, find laughter's friend,
In jokes we find where our troubles end.

Tickling darkness, we shift and sway,
With giggles, the night turns to day.
A twist of fate laced with a pun,
In every shadow, life's laughter's spun.

Let's wrap our worries in humor tight,
And find the spark in the dead of night.
In shadowed corners, a chuckle rings,
With funny bones, we'll sprout our wings.

Jests Beneath the Universe

Under the arch of the endless sky,
We toss our jests like stars, oh my!
A comet sings with a whimsical tune,
While planets giggle beneath the moon.

From galaxies wide to a small café,
Laughter binds us, come what may.
In every corner of the bright expanse,
A punchline waits, inviting our dance.

With a wink and a nudge, we lift our cheer,
Turning life's trials to jests sincere.
Each chuckle shared, a cosmic embrace,
In this grand circus, let humor race.

So savor the moments, the jokes we make,
In the vast universe, we're all awake.
With laughter as our guide, let's play along,
Our spirits high, in a world of song.

Revelations in Whimsy

In a world of jest and play,
We twirl and laugh the night away.
Each giggle tells a tale that's bright,
A twist of fate, a silly sight.

With gnomes and elves that dance around,
We find our joy in silly sounds.
Laughter echoes through the trees,
A symphony of chuckles, please!

From banana peels to whoopee seats,
Life's comic gold is in the beats.
As we stumble with mismatched shoes,
We greet the world, just with a muse.

In every pun that we create,
A spark of joy we celebrate.
We spin our tales through chuckling rhymes,
Unraveling life in silly times.

The Humor of Mortality

Life is but a fleeting jest,
A punchline at its very best.
With every breath, we take our place,
In this grand cosmic, funny race.

We wear our age like clownish hats,
And laugh at life, like silly brats.
A fleeting wink, a playful scoff,
We poke fun at our own back-off.

As candles flicker on each cake,
We joke about the steps we take.
Each moment's laughter, sweet delight,
Makes every dark seem warm and bright.

So let us dance and skip the gloom,
And fill our lives with joy to bloom.
For in the end, it's not the strife,
But laughter that defines our life.

Chuckles Under a Celestial Canopy

Beneath the stars, a funny sight,
Aliens laugh at human plight.
With twinkling eyes, they roll and shake,
At every silly choice we make.

We gaze at clouds that drift on by,
Imagining shapes, oh my, oh my!
With every giggle in the sky,
We paint our dreams, we learn to fly.

A wink from Mars, a grin from Venus,
Our jokes are vast, but none are sinless.
In this cosmos, we find our cheer,
As laughter beams from ear to ear.

So let the stars be our delight,
And fill our hearts with purest light.
Together we will laugh and play,
Embracing life in our own way.

Trivial Pursuits of Joy

With every step, we chase the fun,
In trivial things, our hearts have won.
A board game night, a movie spree,
In every laugh, we feel so free.

From silly hats to puns so bright,
We celebrate the quirks of plight.
Life's little giggles fuel the day,
In playful jest, we choose our way.

A tickle fight, a splashing splash,
We savor each moment, make it last.
When life gets tough, just grab a joke,
And let the laughter be our cloak.

In frivolous quests, we find our zest,
In laughter, we are truly blessed.
For joy is found in every line,
In trivial pursuits, our hearts align.

Joy Unfolding in Tiny Moments

In a world of giggles and glee,
A banana peel waits patiently.
Laughter escapes from the mundane,
As joy floods like a sweet champagne.

A pigeon struts in a fancy hat,
Misguided as it chases a cat.
In the dance of a child's delight,
We find the sun in the darkest night.

A toast to the socks that never pair,
Lost in the dryer, without a care.
Each stumble brings a chuckle bright,
In the chaos, we find pure light.

Life's Quirky Quips

A chicken crossed to make us smile,
With laughter leading all the while.
Every hiccup, a comic scene,
In the laughter, life feels serene.

Why did the lamp break down on its way?
Because it couldn't find its light of day!
Laughter ripples like fresh spring rain,
Washing away our worry and pain.

The snail on the road took a wrong turn,
But in his shell, he found what to learn.
In each quirk, an echo of fate,
We chuckle, and it feels first-rate.

Paradoxes and Punchlines

A wise man once tripped on a stone,
And laughed as he fell, alone.
Wisdom drips from a slip and slide,
Where seriousness takes a ride.

A cat thinks it rules the whole place,
Yet naps through the human race.
In paradoxes, laughter is found,
Beneath the absurd, joy will abound.

The more we plan, the wilder life flows,
As time twirls in unpredictable shows.
With each punchline, uncertainty sways,
In the riddles, we muse for days.

Surreal Humor of Existence

A fish in a hat sat on a bench,
Swapping tales with a wise old wrench.
In the fabric of dreams, we weave,
Absurdities that make us believe.

A giraffe with a neck so long,
Tends to hum the silliest song.
In the fractals of laughter, we roam,
Finding a smile feels just like home.

The clock ticks backward, what a jest,
Making time feel like an unwelcome guest.
Yet through the surreal comedy we dance,
Embracing the chaos, taking a chance.

Punchlines to the Universe

Why did the chicken cross the street?
To show the raccoon it could be neat!
Stars above giggle with glee,
As cosmic jokes dance with esprit.

Life's a jest, a whimsical spree,
Like socks lost in laundry, you see.
With every slip, a chuckle bright,
In the grand sketch, we find the light.

The sun winks down, a perfect tease,
While moonbeams sway like playful leaves.
Through every stumble, laugh and sing,
For joy, my friends, is the real thing.

So here we tread, on this grand stage,
With punchlines jotted on each page.
Let laughter roll and spirits soar,
For humor's key unlocks the door.

Laughing Through the Abyss

In the shadow, a joke takes flight,
Tickling fears in the dead of night.
What did the nihilist say with a grin?
Nothing matters, but let's begin!

The void whispers, with vibes of fun,
Putting frowns to rest, one by one.
A cosmic jest amidst the dark,
Where laughter finds its shining spark.

Wit like stars that flicker and fade,
Can brighten the depths that fear has made.
Why fret and stew, why sit and sigh?
In jest we live; through jest we fly.

So face the abyss with humor's might,
And dance with shadows, feathery light.
Let laughter echo, let spirits lift,
For life's a gift with jokes to sift.

Satire Under the Stars

Beneath the heavens, wisecracks bloom,
As owls converse in the midnight gloom.
Why did the moon refuse to play?
It found the sun too bright to stay!

Planets chuckle at our plight,
Spinning tales in the velvet night.
Each star a wink, a quirky rhyme,
Reflecting the folly of space and time.

What's life without a dose of cheer?
A drudgery, harsh, devoid of clear.
With every quirk, we shape our way,
Crafting laughter at the end of the day.

So as we muse 'neath twinkling skies,
Let satire spark, let humor rise.
For in this jest, our hearts find grace,
In the cosmic dance, our rightful place.

Witty Wanderings

With every step, a quip unfolds,
Life's an adventure where laughter molds.
Why did the grape stop in its track?
It couldn't find its raisin snack!

Through forests lush and valleys deep,
Jokes sprout forth from the roots we keep.
What's a philosopher's favorite drink?
A good 'ol cup of deep thought, I think!

Mountains chuckle, rivers tease,
While breezes hum with playful ease.
Each twist and turn, a riddle made,
Life's a journey, a grand parade.

So let us wander, let us roam,
In laughter's arms, we find our home.
For wit and whimsy light the way,
In every jest, we seize the day.

Revelry and Revelation

In midnight's glow, we chuckle bright,
With silly tales that take their flight.
A pratfall here, a pun over there,
Life's just a joke, if you dare!

With every grin, a truth we find,
In laughter's arms, we're all entwined.
A slip, a trip, we all partake,
In this grand jest, beware the wake!

Like clowns in a ring, we spin and sway,
Each giggle whispers, "Come what may!"
The serious thoughts are tossed aside,
In moments of mirth, we all can glide.

So raise your glass to jovial cheer,
For every chuckle draws us near.
In jest, we dance through night and day,
And find our bliss in a joyful play.

Jests of the Journey

Each step we take, a punchline waits,
With quips and smiles, we navigate.
From road to road, we spin our yarn,
In laughter's shade, no need to warn.

A wobble here, a slip of fate,
Turn life's mishaps to laugh, not hate.
The road may twist, our feet may trip,
Yet joy spills out from every quip.

As travelers bold, we jest and sing,
With joy that makes our spirits spring.
In the silly tales we tell at night,
We find the spark, the pure delight.

So gather 'round, let laughter ring,
Each jest a spark, each giggle a wing.
Together we laugh, our burdens drop,
In this grand parade, we never stop.

Laughter's Lantern

A lantern swings in twilight's haze,
With every giggle, we set ablaze.
A wink, a nod, a jolly jest,
In laughter's warmth, we find our rest.

Through shadows cast, where worries creep,
We sprinkle joy, the heart will leap.
In fumbled words, in playful gleams,
We chase our dreams with silly schemes.

With laughter bright, our path is clear,
Each punchline warm, each chortle dear.
In bumps and grins, we find our shine,
In every jest, our lives align.

So hold that lantern, let it glow,
Through life's wild dance, we'll steal the show.
In humor's light, we stake our claim,
And play this wacky, joyful game.

Whimsical Wonders

In fields of whimsy, laughter blooms,
With playful jests, we chase our dooms.
A twist of fate, a funny face,
In this mad world, we find our pace.

Each bumble brings a chuckle wide,
With joy abound, we take a ride.
Tickling ribs and silly gales,
We write our stories, full of snails!

In jest, we forge our merry way,
With playful hearts, come what may.
Life's a circus, so let it be,
With every laugh, we're truly free.

So let's rejoice and dance along,
To the rhythm of a happy song.
In whimsical wonders, we take our flight,
For this wild ride is pure delight.

The Bright Side of the Infinite

In a universe vast, we laugh a lot,
Finding joy in the space, in every plot.
Stars whisper jokes in the cosmic dance,
While planets giggle, caught in a trance.

We trip over dreams, and memes we share,
Life's a comedy, if you dare.
Tickling our hearts with wits so fine,
Another punchline, and all is divine.

Galaxies spin, but we hold no fear,
Each grin shines brighter, year after year.
The mysteries unfold with a wink and a nod,
In this grand theater where we applaud.

So raise a toast to the clever and kind,
In every riddle, a treasure to find.
With laughter as fuel, we soar through the night,
In every shadow, there's always a light.

Banter Beneath the Surface

Underneath the surface, a jest takes form,
Life's quirks and quibbles keep us warm.
A splash of humor in a tidal wave,
Wit is the light that we all crave.

As the waves crash, our laughter erupts,
Bantering lightly, the universe erupts.
With every wave, we ride the tide,
In humor's embrace, we take in our stride.

Fish swim by with a wink and a grin,
Whispers of jokes in the currents begin.
Plunge into giggles where the waters are bright,
Beneath the surface, everything's light.

So let's share a chuckle and dance in the sea,
Life's a big joke—come laugh with me.
With hearts wide open, we'll dive and explore,
Finding hilarity on every shore.

Lighthearted Philosophies

Philosophers ponder, yet jokes abound,
In laughter and folly, wisdom is found.
Questions asked with a playful jest,
In the realm of humor, we find our rest.

Causality tangled like a ball of string,
Life's quirks reveal what laughter can bring.
Each riddle posed with a twinkle and wink,
Keeps us pondering without a think.

With a giggle, we question the grand and sublime,
Why so serious? Let's laugh for a time!
In the book of existence, turn the page,
With jokes as our guides, we break free from the cage.

So gather your friends, let's laugh 'til we cry,
In lighthearted banter, we'll reach for the sky.
For everything noble can wear a disguise,
A chuckle, a grin—such sweet surprise!

Sighs of Relief and Laughter

When the day gets heavy, just lighten the load,
Share a ridiculous tale on the road.
Sighs of relief in a crowded room,
With laughter like flowers, let troubles bloom.

Comedic timing like a clock on a shelf,
Let's poke some fun at our very own self.
In the chaos of life, find joy in the cracks,
With quirky anecdotes to lighten the facts.

Every stumble is simply a chance to rise,
With giggles and smirks, we enlighten our eyes.
As we pass through the storms, we'll dance in the rain,
With jokes as our umbrella, we lessen the pain.

So join in the laughter, let's skip down the street,
In life's funny moments, our hearts will compete.
With sighs of relief that blossom like spring,
Embrace every chuckle that the universe brings.

Verses Wrapped in Humor

In a world where chaos reigns,
Laughter chases after pains.
Jokes like balloons, up they fly,
Tickling thoughts as they drift by.

With each pun, the sun does shine,
Making frowns turn to a line.
Life's a jest, a playful dance,
Join the fun, and take a chance.

In silly hats and mismatched shoes,
We find joy in being fools.
Each punchline is a twinkling star,
Guiding us, no matter how far.

So let's toast with cola and cheer,
To the giggles we hold dear.
Life's a circus, come enjoy the show,
Laughter's free, let it overflow.

Lighthearted Legends of Life

Once a chicken crossed the road,
To share its tale, a lightened load.
"Why'd I cross?" it laughed with glee,
"To get to the other side, you see!"

In gardens where the daisies bloom,
We chuckle at life's quirky room.
A sneeze can send a cat in flight,
Turning calm to frantic fright.

The mailman trips, the dog gives chase,
Life's a race without a pace.
In every slip, there's joy to find,
A playful spark in heart and mind.

So gather 'round, let laughter reign,
In goofy tales, there's little pain.
We dance through days with silly grace,
Finding smiles in every place.

Jests that Shape Reality

A wise man said with a twist of fate,
"Life's a joke, don't take the bait."
With laughter echoing high and low,
We brighten shadows, watch them grow.

A cat in boots, a fish that sings,
Funny musings that laughter brings.
Dancing in the rain, we splash,
Turning woes into a silly dash.

When life hands you a twisty lime,
Make a drink and sip in time.
For every frown that tries to speak,
A giggle can resolve the peak.

In jests we see the light so clear,
Wit's a gift, let's spread the cheer.
Life's absurd, but it's a thrill,
Let laughter echo, stay fulfilled.

The Artistry of Absurdity

In a world of wobbly chairs,
We find the joy that boldly dares.
A cow once dreamed of flight and grace,
Jumped over moons with cheeky face.

With every chuckle, colors blend,
Absurdity becomes the best friend.
When logic bends like silly putty,
We laugh till our brains feel all nutty.

The pancake flipped, it sails so high,
While squirrels plot conspiracy in the sky.
Life's a canvas, painted bright,
With every stroke, we find delight.

So wear those socks that don't quite match,
Embrace the chaos, make a catch.
For laughter breathes the sweetest art,
And funny moments fill the heart.

Comedic Reflections

In the mirror, I see my face,
Each wrinkle tells a silly case.
Laughter's the cure for all our trials,
It makes the hardest moments smile.

A chicken crossed the road, they say,
To find the punchline on the way.
With every giggle, we can unwind,
Jokes are the treasures we hope to find.

Life's a game of jest and tease,
Tickling ribs with whimsical ease.
So let's not take it all to heart,
Embrace the laughs, that's the real art.

In every stumble, trip, and fall,
There's humor waiting, after all.
So toast to jesters, big and small,
Together we stand, we'll never stall.

Punchlines in the Cosmos

Stars twinkle like jesters in the night,
Bringing laughter with their light.
Planets spin with a cheeky grin,
In this vast stage where jokes begin.

Aliens watch our Earthly strife,
They chuckle at our busy life.
With every blunder, they shake their heads,
As we tumble, roll, and leap from beds.

Galaxies play hide and seek,
As comets race with humor sleek.
Wormholes twist with a punchline tight,
In cosmic giggles, we find our light.

In this universe where we all belong,
Each laugh is rhythmic, like a song.
So reach for stars, let laughter flow,
And dance beneath the cosmic glow.

Giggles Beneath Stardust

In the dust of stars, we twirl and sway,
Chasing giggles, come what may.
With every wink and cheeky snort,
We find joy in a cosmic court.

Moonbeams shimmer, a playful jest,
Whispering secrets that we know best.
Life's a stage, where laughter's queen,
In every moment, joy is seen.

Clouds drift by with a laugh or two,
Painting skies in shades of blue.
Let's leap through puddles, skip through time,
For every giggle is a wondrous rhyme.

As stardust settles on our shoes,
We trip through laughter, lose the blues.
In silly moments, treasures hide,
Let's find them all, side by side.

Serendipity in Silly Moments

Serendipity dances in the rain,
A puddle forms, a playful gain.
With every splash, we burst with glee,
In silly moments, wild and free.

Unexpected turns around each bend,
Life's a joke, and we're the trend.
With each mishap and quirky fail,
We pen our stories, laughter's trail.

A banana peel or a slip of fate,
Brings out the giggles, it's never late.
So let's embrace mischief, leave behind,
The serious thoughts that clog the mind.

In every jest, there's joy to find,
We strut through life, a merry kind.
Let's celebrate the wild and bold,
For every laugh is a story told.

Curiosities in Comedy

Why did the chicken cross the street?
To get to the punchline, that's neat.
Laughter rides on every whim,
With each quip, our spirits brim.

Time bends with a joke in hand,
Turning frowns to laughter so grand.
In quirks and quirks, wisdom hides,
Finding joy where humor abides.

A ticklish thought, a silly cheer,
Life's absurdity, crystal clear.
With laughter, we conquer strife,
Each jest a slice of vibrant life.

So roll with giggles, let them flow,
In punchlines, deeper truths we know.
Curiosities weave the tale,
Comedy's embrace, we'll never fail.

Tales of Timeless Tickle

A fish and a clown both had a bet,
Who'd tell the best joke, you can place your set.
The fish flopped around, with scales so bright,
While the clown splashed laughs like stars at night.

Beneath the waves, they'd tangle and tease,
Crafting snickers that ride the breeze.
With every chuckle, wisdom unfurls,
In silly stories, life twirls and twirls.

To tickle the mind, to poke and prod,
In laughter's light, we find the odd.
Each tale a ripple, each giggle a wave,
In timeless humor, we're all a bit brave.

So gather 'round with a grin so wide,
In jest, we find joy we cannot hide.
Tales unfold in every quirk,
Tickling hearts, where laughter works.

The Gags of Gaia

Nature chuckles as trees sway low,
Whispering secrets only squirrels know.
The sun cracks jokes as it rises bright,
Painting the sky in hues of delight.

Clouds get good laughs, they puff and morph,
Turning into poodles, then back to a dwarf.
On rooftops, kids giggle with glee,
As raindrops dance in a whimsical spree.

With every rustle, the grasses sing,
Mirth blooms like flowers in the ring.
Gaia's humor, so fresh and bold,
In every leaf, a story unfolds.

So let's ride the winds in joyful flight,
Embrace the world, both day and night.
In the gags of Gaia, life's a show,
With laughter's warmth, we gracefully flow.

Mischief and Meaning in Motion

A cat in a hat danced on the floor,
With mischief tucked in every paw's core.
Swinging to rhythms only cats know,
Sprinkling giggles like confetti's glow.

In playful leaps, we chase the sun,
Finding humor in races we run.
With each stumble, laughter erupts,
Life's sweetest nectar, in joy, we sup.

Bursts of giggles in a juggling act,
Where meanings twist with every impact.
Motion and mirth, a delightful frieze,
In the chaos, we find the keys.

So let's twirl amidst the laughter and fun,
Embrace the quirks, each foolish run.
In mischief's dance, wisdom we gain,
Life's too short, let's play with the rain.

Laughing with the Universe

Stars twinkle like laughter, so bright,
Planets spin in pure delight.
Galaxies dance in cosmic play,
Who knew space could joke this way?

Comets zoom by with a grin,
Asteroids chuckle, let the fun begin.
Each supernova, a burst of cheer,
In this vast expanse, humor is near.

Black holes whisper silly tales,
Of time travel mishaps and epic fails.
The cosmos grins, it's plain to see,
Life's grand jest is shared with glee.

Embrace the cosmos, join the jest,
In this universe, we're all a guest.
So laugh with stars, forget your strife,
For humor is the spark of life.

Joyful Ironies in the Everyday

Traffic jams and coffee spills,
Life's little quirks bring silly thrills.
A cat who thinks it's a dog,
Or lost keys under a froggy bog.

The plants that wilt with too much love,
Mismatched socks from the dryer, oh so tough.
A boss who can't find where they're at,
While the office clock's a lazy brat.

Umbrellas flipped inside out, oh dear,
Raindrops dancing, but we shed no tear.
Life serves pepper, we sprinkle in salt,
With every misstep, we laugh at the vault.

Embrace the irony in the mundane,
For laughter's the sunshine after the rain.
With every quirk, our spirits soar,
In life's comedy, we yearn for more.

The Serendipity of Silliness

Trip on a shoelace, what a scene,
Fall into laughter, it's quite routine.
The joy of surprise in the little things,
A joke that life and laughter brings.

A squirrel that dances on the street,
With acorns in hand, it's quite a feat.
A dog wearing glasses, quite a sight,
Life's silly moments feel just right.

Forgotten birthdays turn into fun,
With cake on your face, joy has begun.
A hedge that looks like a grumpy face,
Nature's humor transcends all space.

In every stumble, in every fall,
Life's a comedy, we all can recall.
So find the laughter in what you do,
For silliness connects me and you.

A Funny Bone Awakening

Woke up to find my shirt inside out,
A fashion statement, there's no doubt.
Coffee spills in the morning sun,
Rivers of laughter have just begun.

Neighbors wrestling their dogs on the lawn,
A showdown of fur, their patience gone.
With each bark and tumble, spirits lift high,
Who knew life's battles could be so spry?

Dad's jokes that make us collectively groan,
Yet somehow, they feel like home.
A pun that lands like a dodgeball throw,
In this family game, we steal the show.

So take a moment, embrace the odd,
Life's quirks are the treasures we applaud.
Let your funny bone guide your way,
For laughter is the best part of our day.

Endlessly Amusing Explorations

In the circus of existence, we laugh and play,
Chasing shadows that dance in a merry display.
Punchlines whisper secrets, tickling the mind,
In this wild, wacky world, hilarities unwind.

Juggling our worries, spinning dreams in the air,
A grin is the compass, guiding us with flair.
Laughter like confetti, it fills up the skies,
Every chuckle a star, as the cosmos replies.

Funny hats and odd socks, who says we must fit?
Embrace the chaos, let's laugh at the skit.
In every misstep, there's humor, you see,
Life's quirks make us giggle, set our spirits free.

So here we stand, with smiles wide and bright,
In this carnival of joy, we dance through the night.
Collecting life's quirks, like treasures of gold,
Each joke a reminder, let your heart be bold.

The Amusement of Adventure

Why did the chicken cross the cosmic road?
To quack at the universe, and lighten the load.
In every twist and turn, let laughter ignite,
A journey of fun, every day a delight.

With maps made of whimsy, we wander and roam,
Filling our hearts with the laughter of home.
Take a leap into silliness, dance with the breeze,
Each moment a riddle, meant to please.

When life hands you lemons, just make jokes instead,
Sprinkle joy like confetti, let laughter spread.
Through valleys of puns, and mountains of cheer,
Adventure grows richer, the more we steer clear.

So strap on your humor, let's venture afar,
In this grand amusement, we're all shining stars.
Every chuckle a bridge, every smile a compass,
Join hands in the fun, let's create a big ruckus!

Cosmic Quips and Cosmic Questions

What's the secret of stars? They twinkle and tease,
Bouncing jokes off planets, causing ripples with ease.
In the humor of space, we find solace and grace,
Infinite laughter echoes through time and through space.

Do aliens giggle at life's little quirks?
Do they ponder our jokes, or just think we're jerks?
In the vastness of void, there's always a jest,
A cosmic reminder that laughter's the best.

Planets spin slowly, yet time's moving fast,
In this whirlpool of riddles, let's never look past.
The wonders we share, with whimsy in tow,
Each question a riddle, each answer a show.

So gaze at the night, with a grin on your face,
In the tapestry woven, we all have a place.
With cosmic hilarities, our souls intertwined,
In this grand comedy, the universe is kind.

Jokes in the Space Between

In silence the stars start to laugh,
Their twinkles ring out like a gaffe.
A comet slips, with a grin so wide,
Spilling laughter across the night tide.

Asteroids dance in a cosmic ballet,
Gravities pulling them into play.
Between planets, Mirth has its reign,
While black holes devour the mundane.

Each quasar whispers a ticklish spark,
Echoing giggles through the dark.
Light-years apart, humor's our voice,
In the void, we always rejoice.

What is life if not a jest,
A cosmic riddle we try our best?
With every punchline, we take a leap,
In the universe's arms, laughter is deep.

Smiles that Stretch Across Time

From ancient scripts to memes so grand,
Humor jogs through every land.
A Pharaoh chuckles from his tomb,
While time-worn jesters still resume.

In every era, a punchline rings,
As history laughs at trivial things.
With jesters' tales and puns so spry,
We weave our laughter as years fly by.

Future's bright with clever quips,
While past gives jokes that make us flip.
Across all ages, wit's the glue,
Binding us in chuckles anew.

So here's to moments shared in mirth,
Creating smiles that know no dearth.
Whispers of laughter through space and time,
In every heart, a giggle sublime.

Cosmic Chuckles

Galaxies spin with a cheeky laugh,
Stars throw jokes like a playful gaffe.
In the void where silence would reign,
Comets crack wise, and never complain.

Pulsars pulse with comic timing,
Dancing photons always shining.
In the universe's grand design,
Wit and wonder together align.

Nebulas swirl with laughter and light,
Creating chaos that's pure delight.
Each black hole's a cosmic punchline,
Sucking in woes, leaving joy divine.

So let's float through this endless space,
With humor and heart, we've found our place.
In every star, a chuckle awaits,
Cosmic connections, oh how it elates!

Wit in the Wilderness

Among the trees, laughter does spring,
Nature's humor takes to wing.
Squirrels play tricks and rabbits jest,
In this wild realm, they're truly blessed.

The brook bubbles joyously along,
Sharing secrets in a merry song.
Wit hides in bushes, ready to pounce,
While owls perch, with wisdom to flounce.

Every rustle carries a playful tease,
As leaves giggle in the gentle breeze.
Mountains chuckle with each echo loud,
Nature's canvas is rich and proud.

So speak to the winds, let your heart sing,
In wild abandon, find the zing.
Wit in the wilderness, alive and bright,
Crafts a joyful world, pure and light.

Tickles of Time and Space

In a world where laughter reigns,
We find joy in silly gains.
A tickle here, a giggle there,
Life's a joke, if you dare.

Floating through the cosmic dance,
Each moment's worth a hearty chance.
With puns that echo through the void,
We find the fun that can't be toyed.

Chronicles of chuckles unfold,
In every story, a twist retold.
Witty whispers weave the day,
In every laugh, a bright bouquet.

Forget the worries, keep it light,
With jests that twinkle in the night.
For every stumble, a new delight,
Tickles and grins make wrong seem right.

The Lighthearted Path

On pathways paved with playful cheer,
We stroll along without a fear.
Where every misstep sparks a grin,
The dance of life, where laughs begin.

A joke, a pun, a quirky say,
Guides us through the light of day.
With every turn, a gag appears,
We walk with joy, releasing fears.

Through fields of smiles and playful sighs,
We chase the sun, as laughter flies.
In simple moments, wisdom lies,
Life's a jest that never dies.

So take a step, and let it flow,
Embrace the fun, enjoy the show.
With hearts so light, we skip and hop,
Finding joy that never stops.

Nuances of Nonsense

In realms where nonsense reigns supreme,
We chase the thread of every dream.
With whimsy woven into each thought,
The laughter comes, no need for fraught.

Absurdity is the name of the game,
In wacky tales, we stake our claim.
With every riddle, a chuckle hides,
Revealing joy where nonsense bides.

Life's puzzle pieces often stray,
But jokes align and lead the way.
In quirky corners, wisdom sits,
Wrapped in laughter, life's comic wits.

So join the dance, embrace the jest,
In playful chaos, we find our rest.
For in the silly, the wise converge,
In nuances of nonsense, we'll emerge.

Quirk and Quandary

A twist of fate in every day,
With quirky thoughts that come to play.
In puzzles wrapped in laughter's embrace,
We find solutions with a smile on our face.

When life becomes a tangled string,
A joke can make the laughter ring.
With every quandary, a chance to jest,
In quirkiness, we find our zest.

Through silly contradictions we roam,
In a world where humor finds a home.
With every mischief, joy ignites,
In quirky tales, our heart delights.

So let's embrace the quirks we find,
In silly challenges, laughter's kind.
With every giggle, we'll take the leap,
In quirk and quandary, our spirits keep.

Whimsy on Life's Rollercoaster

Life's a ride, with ups and downs,
Each twist a chance to lose our frowns.
We laugh at loops, we scream with glee,
In every turn, there's joy, you'll see.

A clown pops up, and we all cheer,
With silly hats and jokes to share.
Hold on tight, don't lose your snack,
On this wild ride, there's no turning back!

So take a breath, enjoy the show,
Life's a circus, go with the flow.
The ticket's free, the fun's in sight,
In every giggle, find delight.

So let your heart embrace the whimsy,
For life's a plot, both strange and flimsy.
With each chuckle, we'll sail along,
To the rhythm of our cheerful song.

Mirth's Journey through Existence

We wander through this grand bazaar,
With silly rabbits and a dancing star.
Each step we take, a funny story,
In absurdity, we find our glory.

A jester's hat, a playful tease,
Life giggles softly in the breeze.
With every stumble, we learn to jest,
In the folly, we find our rest.

A punchline here, a quip in time,
Each witty thought, a little rhyme.
So on this journey, laugh with me,
In the silliness, we are free.

Mirth is the compass guiding our way,
In every chuckle, come what may.
We embrace the quirks, the quirks are bliss,
In the comedy of life, we find our kiss.

The Agile Dance of Irony

In the dance of life, we spin around,
With steps both silly, and often unbound.
Irony leads with a wink and a nod,
In this dance, we move like a flawed god.

A misstep here, a laugh erupts,
As we twirl, life's laughter interrupts.
Each faux pas becomes a funny tale,
With wobbly feet, we set our sail.

So take my hand, let's trip in style,
With every giggle, we stretch our smile.
In life's ballet, with grace or clumsily,
We find our rhythm, at last, humbly.

Oh, the sprightly jig of sweet irony,
In every mischief, we find our glee.
With every misstep under the moon's glow,
In this playful dance, we'll steal the show.

A Symphony of Chuckles

In the hall of laughs, we gather round,
A symphony of giggles can be found.
With each note struck, a joke takes flight,
In this concert, everything feels right.

The maestro waves, a wink and a grin,
As jokes and laughter all begin.
The audience chuckles, a thunderous blend,
In each melody, our spirits mend.

So bring your puns, your quirks, your cheer,
Join in the fun, let's all persevere.
In harmony, we sway, we sing,
Life's greatest joys, the laughter we bring.

With every chuckle, the world feels bright,
In this symphony, we dance through the night.
So lift your voice, let joy resound,
In this orchestra of life, love is found.

Smiles Wrapped in Stardust

In a universe so wide,
We burst with laughter inside.
Jokes twinkle like stars at night,
Sprinkling joy, oh what a sight.

A giggle from the cosmic breeze,
Life's punchlines come with such ease.
Each chuckle spins a tale untold,
With warmth and humor, we are bold.

Like comets flying past the moon,
Laughter sings a happy tune.
In the chaos, we find our spark,
As jokes dance wildly in the dark.

So gather 'round, let's share the glee,
In each jest, we find the key.
Wrapped in stardust, hearts unite,
Floating on joy, we take flight.

Comedic Ripples in Time

Time trickles like a playful stream,
Life's quirks ignite a silly dream.
The clock ticks with a wily grin,
As laughter bubbles deep within.

Yesterday's fumble, today's jest,
Each misstep turns into a fest.
With jokes as ripples on the pond,
We dance through life, carefree and fond.

A slip, a trip, a hearty laugh,
Life's playful math creates the path.
We navigate with comic ease,
Finding joy in every tease.

So let each moment spark delight,
As comedy dances in the light.
With laughter echoing through the halls,
We celebrate the fun that calls.

The Dance of Absurdity

Absurdity weaves a quirky lace,
With silly faces, we embrace.
In the waltz of life's wild show,
Each twirl bursts with laughter's glow.

Frogs in bow ties, cats with hats,
Life's strange humor, all of that.
We trip on wisdom, trip on bliss,
In every fumble, a silly kiss.

So let's tango with the bizarre,
And watch the world go a little far.
With every giggle, we pirouette,
In comedy's arms, there's no regret.

Embrace the dance and let it flow,
With joy and whimsy on the go.
The rhythm of laughter, perfectly timed,
In this crazy ballet, we are primed.

Witty Reflections of Reality

Reality's mirror holds a jest,
With winks and chuckles, we're impressed.
A wink here, a pun there,
In life's riddle, humor's rare.

Glancing in, what do we see?
A world spun with irony.
Moments cracked and slightly torn,
Gags and goofs are how we're born.

Funny hats and glasses round,
The absurdities we've found.
In quirky truths, we find delight,
As laughter takes its rightful flight.

So let us raise a toast tonight,
To wisdom wrapped in sheer delight.
With witty lines to guide our way,
We'll laugh anew, come what may.

Humor and Heartbeats

Laughter bounces in the air,
Tickling hearts without a care.
Each chuckle adds a little zest,
Finding joy in every jest.

Frog in a hat, what a sight!
Dancing till the morning light.
Life's a stage, let's play our part,
With giggles glowing in the heart.

Slipping on banana peels,
Truth revealed in silly feels.
Every stumble shares a grin,
In this game, we all can win.

So chase the shadows, watch them flee,
For in each joke, we all are free.
As belly laughs bring forth delight,
We dance together, pure and bright.

The Paradox of Joy

Here's a riddle full of cheer,
Why did the chicken disappear?
To the other side, it quietly crept,
Where all the happy folks laughed and leapt.

Life's a dance, a wobbly jig,
With a cat in a hat doing a gig.
Every misstep leads us to glee,
Who knew a fall could set us free?

Jokes bounce like a rubber ball,
Echoing in the silences tall.
In every pun, there's wisdom hid,
Laughter, a gift we've all amid.

From ticklish toes to snorts so loud,
Joy wears a face that's not too proud.
In paradox, we find our voice,
In laughter, we rejoice our choice.

Quips at the Crossroads

At the crossroads, choices sprout,
A squirrel pondered, 'What's this about?'
Should I go left or take the right?
But oh, he slipped and took to flight!

Life's a circus, a grand old show,
With clowns and acrobats in tow.
Every jibe and silly prank,
Leaves us smiling as we tank.

A thunderstorm of jests and puns,
Bubbles of laughter, breaking runs.
At every corner, joy awaits,
As humor dances, unlocking gates.

So take a chance, embrace the jest,
Life is best when we're at our jest.
With every punchline, a glimpse so bright,
At the crossroads, we find our light.

Mirth Amongst Mysteries

In shadows deep, where whispers play,
A riddle hides, but it won't stay.
A ghost once laughed, with a wink so sly,
And tricked us all with a pie in the sky.

Hidden beneath the stars so wide,
Laughter blooms where secrets hide.
In cosmic jokes with ancient themes,
Life's a riddle wrapped in dreams.

Who knew that ducks with shoes could strut?
In every flap, we find what's cut.
Mysteries unravel with each good pun,
In the end, we're all just having fun!

So join the dance, embrace the jest,
In laughter's arms, we find our rest.
Mirth amidst mysteries sweetly sways,
Guiding us through these zany days.

Laughter: The Invisible Thread

In a world where giggles shift,
Joyful pranks give spirits lift.
A wink, a word, the crowd erupts,
As silly joys, they gladly interrupt.

We craft our tales with silly flair,
Turning frowns into fresh air.
With each chuckle, hearts entwine,
A thread of laughter, pure and fine.

In every quirk, a spark ignites,
Life's oddities bring sweet delights.
A dance of humor, light as air,
A cosmic joke, everywhere.

So let's embrace the playful jest,
In life's riddle, we feel blessed.
With every smile, we shape our day,
In laughter's grasp, we find our way.

Playful Parables and Punchlines

Once upon a punchline bright,
A ticklish tale takes flight at night.
A twist of fate, a whimsy twist,
In jokes, we find the things we missed.

The wise ones chuckle, share their lore,
With puns and stories, never a bore.
Each nugget wrapped in laughter's glow,
Unfolds a truth we all can know.

Around the table, smiles unwind,
As humor weaves through every mind.
Life's curiosities, a funny game,
Parables that never stay the same.

So gather round, and share a laugh,
For joy is found in the aftermath.
In every jest, a lesson clear,
A playful heart draws all things near.

Joking with the Divine

Oh cosmic jester, what a sight,
You toss the stars with pure delight.
In every quirk, we feel your play,
As life unfolds in shades of gray.

Among the clouds, your giggles rise,
In every moment, joy implies.
With every stumble, there's a grin,
In sacred mischief, we dive in.

The universe winks, a sly surprise,
In whispered jokes, your humor lies.
Each giggle echoes in the night,
In laughter's name, all feels so right.

So let us dance on stardust beams,
And weave our hopes into our dreams.
With every jest, a truth divine,
In playful moments, hearts align.

The Art of Amusing Existence

In the gallery of dreams we roam,
Laughter's portrait feels like home.
Each brushstroke casts a joyful spell,
A masterpiece where stories dwell.

Through life's canvas, colors splash,
In every joke, emotions clash.
We paint the world with shades of cheer,
In every giggle, love draws near.

With irony draped upon the walls,
Humor echoes, and laughter calls.
A dance of whimsy on the stage,
In funny tales, we turn the page.

So feast on joy, our hearts' great feast,
In amusing tales, we find our peace.
Through laughter's lens, we see the light,
In this artful life, all feels right.

The Comedian's Guide to Being

In a world of things to ponder,
Find the jests that help you wander.
Smile at chaos, dance with glee,
Life's a stage, and you're the marquee.

Crack a pun or tell a tale,
Let your laughter never fail.
A punchline here, a quip just right,
You'll shine brighter than the night.

Serious moments, oh beware,
A ticklish twist will fill the air.
Banter and jest in all you seek,
Laughter's magic makes us unique.

So grab a joke, let it roll free,
Open your heart, let humor be.
In every giggle, joy you'll find,
The secrets of the human mind.

Sips of Laughter

Pour a glass of bubbling cheer,
Savor wit, let joy draw near.
Each sip a giggle, a hearty grin,
With every chuckle, let life begin.

Chase away the heavy fog,
With whiff and chortle, dance like a dog.
Sip the wit of friends around,
In every drop, pure joy is found.

A hearty laugh, a little jest,
Is better than all the rest.
Glasses raised to humor grand,
In laughter's grip, we take a stand.

So let's toast to joy we share,
With each tickle, let's declare:
Life is sweeter with laughter's lace,
A cozy rib-tickling embrace.

Life's Elixir

Stirring laughter in a bowl,
A sprinkle of silliness makes us whole.
Mix it with mirth and a hearty cheer,
This potion of joy will steer you clear.

Take a shot at the daily grind,
With giggles and gaffes, you will find.
A sip of joy, a splash of fun,
Each dose helps all worries run.

Chuckle like a child, so pure,
In this elixir, life's secure.
Raise your glass to the friendliest jest,
For laughter is truly life's best quest.

So let's concoct this bubbly brew,
With every giggle, we're born anew.
Life's finest flavors arise in the light,
When we sip laughter day and night.

Mirth Amidst the Mundane

In the humdrum of our days,
Find a giggle in so many ways.
Turn chores to comedy, wipe those frowns,
With silly tricks, you'll win those crowns.

A spilled drink, a playful flop,
Life's mishaps make the best backdrop.
Smirk at struggles as they unfold,
For humor is worth more than gold.

When life gets dull, pull out a grin,
Guffaws will help keep the joy within.
Search for smiles in the routine race,
Mirth's embrace is a warm embrace.

Amidst the dull, let jests align,
With laughter's charge, you will shine.
Life's a tapestry of goofy fun,
In every thread, a smile is spun.

Cosmic Chuckles and Giggles

In the vastness of the sky so blue,
Even stars have jokes for you.
Planets spin in a dance so grand,
While comets leave laughter on their strand.

Galaxies twinkle, sharing glee,
While the moon grins down playfully.
The sun winks bright, a heavenly jest,
In the cosmos, humor is the best.

Black holes laughing at time and space,
Wormholes tickling at a dizzying pace.
Laughter echoes through cosmic streams,
Life's ridiculous in all our dreams.

So float apart in the cosmic sea,
With every giggle, feel free to be.
Treasure the quips the universe flings,
In the grand design, laughter sings.

www.ingramcontent.com/pod-product-compliance
Ingram Content Group UK Ltd.
Pitfield, Milton Keynes, MK11 3LW, UK
UKHW010436170125
4146UKWH00047B/170